The FADE OUT

Sebastian Girner - Editorial Coordinator

Thanks to Amy Condit.

MEDIA INQUIRIES SHOULD BE DIRECTED TO UTA - Agents Julien Thuan and Geoff Morley

THE FADE OUT: ACT TWO. First printing. September 2015. Contains material originally published in magazine form as THE FADE OUT #5-8.

ISBN: 978-1-63215-447-7

Published by Image Comics, Inc. Office of publication: 2001 Center Street, 6th Floor, Berkeley, CA, 94704.

Publication design by Sean Phillips

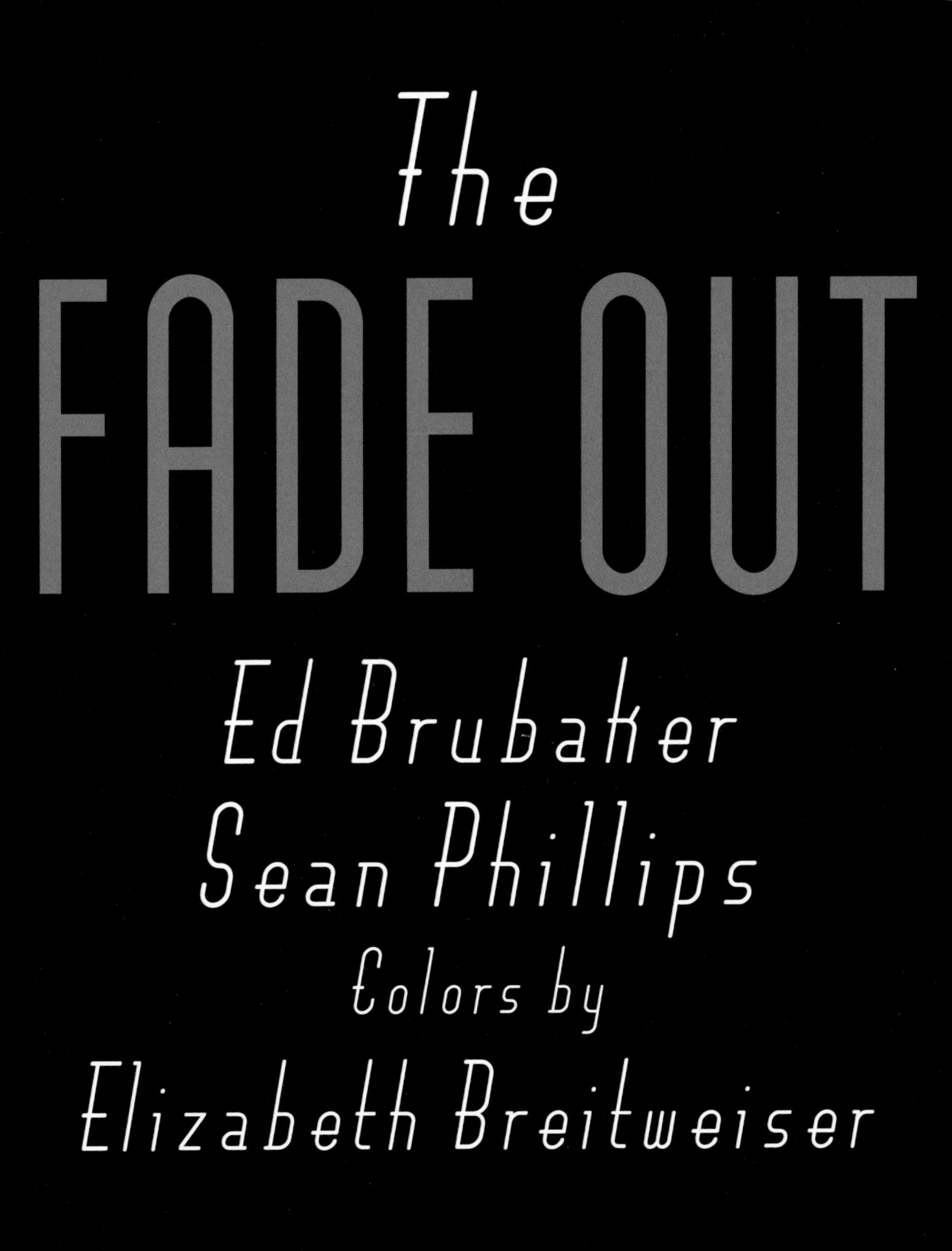
The
FADE OUT
Ed Brubaker
Sean Phillips
Colors by
Elizabeth Breitweiser

Act Two

Cast Of Characters

GIL MASON
Blacklisted Screenwriter

CHARLIE PARISH
Screenwriter Fronting for a Blacklisted Friend

AL KAMP
Co-Founder of Victory Street Pictures

PHIL BRODSKY
Studio Security Chief

FRANZ SCHMITT
German Expatriate Director

VALERIA SOMMERS
Murdered Starlet

DOTTIE QUINN
Studio PR Girl

MAYA SILVER
Valeria's Replacement

TYLER GRAVES
Hollywood Heart-throb

JACK "FLAPJACK" JONES
Former Child Star

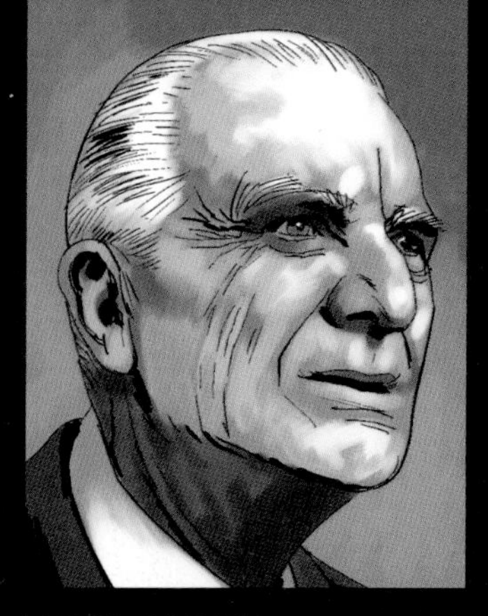

VICTOR THURSBY
Co-Founder of Victory Street Pictures

DASHIELL HAMMETT
Famous Crime Writer

MELBA MASON
Gil's Whip-smart Wife

EARL RATH
Dashing Movie Star

ARMANDO LOPEZ
Big Band Trumpet Player

The Broken Ones

YOU WANNA KNOW MY PROBLEM WITH CAPITALISM?
GIL WAS FEELING GOOD, EVEN THOUGH HE SHOULDN'T HAVE BEEN.
BUT HE WAS THREE DRINKS INTO THE NIGHT...
IT DOESN'T ACCOUNT FOR PEOPLE BEING IGNORANT FUCKING HILLBILLIES...
...AND TWENTY BUCKS UP FROM THE POKER TABLE IN THE BACK ROOM.
EVERY MOVIE GETS STEERED TOWARDS WHAT PEOPLE SUPPOSEDLY WANT...
BUT THEY ALL WANT THE SAME DUMB BULLSHIT...
THEY JUST DON'T KNOW ANY BETTER.
SEE, WITH ART, YOU GOTTA GIVE PEOPLE WHAT THEY NEED... NOT WHAT THEY WANT.
STILL, HE SHOULD HAVE KNOWN SOMETHING WAS BOUND TO BURST HIS BUBBLE.
SOUNDS KINDA CONDESCENDING TO ME...

...BUT WHAT DO I KNOW?
I'M JUST ONE OF THE MINDLESS *PROLETARIAT*.

PHIL BRODSKY, HEAD OF SECURITY FOR THE STUDIO.
JESUS, THEY SENT THE BIG MAN *HIMSELF*...
GIL HADN'T BEEN EXPECTING THAT.
WHERE'S THE OLD MAN?

IN THE BACK... CORNER BOOTH, WITH SOME *B-GIRL*.

TAKE CARE OF IT, BOYS.

SO, *GIL MASON*...
LOOKS LIKE YOU'RE A REAL "*WRONG PLACE, WRONG TIME*" KINDA GUY, DOESN'T IT?

GIL THOUGHT THAT ACTUALLY COULD SUM UP HIS LIFE... BUT HE KNEW THERE WAS ANOTHER FACTOR IN PLAY, TOO...
THAT HE WAS HERE BY CHOICE, NOT ACCIDENT.
GIL PUT HIMSELF IN THE WRONG PLACES ALL THE TIME... IT WAS HIS WORST BAD HABIT.
CHARLIE'S FILM HAD COME NORTH TO OJAI FOR MORE RESHOOTS.
VICTORY STREET CO-FOUNDER AL KAMP HAD A BIG RANCH UP HERE, WHERE THEY MOSTLY SHOT WESTERNS NOW.
BUT THERE WERE STILL SOME STANDING SETS FROM THE ONE-REELERS KAMP HAD MADE HIS FORTUNE PRODUCING BACK IN THE '20s...
THE KRAZY KIDS... TUTTLE AND MARTY... SKINNY CARMICHAEL...

THEY'D BE SHOOTING ON THE "SMALL TOWN MAIN STREET" SET FOR A FEW DAYS...
AND THE "MOUNTAIN CABIN HIDEOUT" FOR ANOTHER FEW.
MENS' FURNISHINGS
CITIZEN'S
ATIONAL BANK

THIS MEANT GIL HAD TO GO NORTH, TOO...
SO HE COULD BE NEARBY FOR REWRITES.
CHARLIE HAD TOLD HIM TO STAY AT THE MOTEL AND WAIT FOR HIS CALL...
AND HE KNEW THAT WAS THE SMART THING TO DO.
BUT NO... GIL HAD TO GO TO THE BAR DOWN THE ROAD INSTEAD.

HE'D FOLDED ON A STRAIGHT THERE, THE LAST TIME THEY'D BEEN UP THIS WAY...
AND IT HAD BEEN EATING AT HIM EVER SINCE.
OTOR
ODGE

ONE HAND, WHAT CAN IT HURT? HE TOLD HIMSELF... NO ONE KNOWS ME HERE.
BUT IT WAS NEVER JUST ONE HAND, OR JUST ONE DRINK.
I'LL RAISE IT A FIN...
SO HE WAS STILL AT THAT TABLE WHEN AL KAMP HIMSELF CAME WANDERING IN, ALREADY STINKING DRUNK...
OH, MISTER KAMP... HOW NICE TO HAVE YOU BACK...
HE SHOULD HAVE LEFT RIGHT THEN, BUT THE TROUBLE-MAGNET INSIDE JUST WOULDN'T LET HIM.
I'M OUT.
EVERYONE HAD HEARD THE RUMORS ABOUT KAMP'S MENTAL STATE BEFORE HIS RETIREMENT...
NOT YOU, THE OTHER ONE...
BUT SEEING IT FIRSTHAND, GIL COULDN'T LOOK AWAY.
ARE YOU SURE, SIR? I KNOW A LOT OF THINGS SHE DOESN'T...

IT WAS MEN LIKE THIS WHO HAD RUINED HIM.
YOU DON'T TOUCH ME, BITCH! I TOUCH YOU!

AND NOW HERE THE OLD MAN WAS, SLAPPING AROUND B-GIRLS...
DEMANDING A YOUNGER MODEL.
NOW GET ME THE OTHER ONE!

FITZGERALD HAD BEEN RIGHT WHEN HE SAID "THE RICH WERE DIFFERENT THAN US," GIL THOUGHT...

BUT THEY END JUST LIKE THE REST OF US, SITTING IN THEIR OWN PISS, WONDERING WHERE ALL THEIR TIME WENT.

SO GIL WATCHED A SENILE OLD DRUNK BRAG ABOUT HIMSELF TO A GIRL WHO WAS BEING PAID TO LISTEN...
...AND SKINNY... HELL, I MADE UP HIS WHOLE GODDAMN ACT FOR HIM...

AND FOR THE FIRST TIME IN YEARS, HE FELT THERE MIGHT ACTUALLY BE SOME JUSTICE IN THIS WORLD...

...UNTIL PHIL BRODSKY SHOWED UP.
THINK YOU AN' ME BETTER GO FOR A RIDE, PAL.

CITIZEN'S
NATIONAL BANK
Just understand this, kitten... There are lines that you cross that you can't uncross again...
I know what I want.
No, you don't.
NATIONAL BANK
If you do this, you won't be the same girl who went into that bank when we come back out.
Good. I don't want to be.
That girl might as well not have lived at all... Just a scared little mouse of a girl.
I don't want to be her anymore, darling... Not one tiny bit.

CITIZENS NATIONAL BANK
All right then... Let's go rob a bank.
After you.
...JUST A SCARED LITTLE MOUSE OF A GIRL.
BUT I WANT OUT OF THAT CAGE, DARLING... I WANT OUT.
CITIZEN'S NATIONAL BANK
OKAY THEN... LET'S GO GET RICH, WHY DON'T WE?
I THOUGHT YOU'D NEVER ASK.
CUT! FUCKING CUT!

THIS IS *SHIT*.
YOU DON'T HAVE TO TELL ME, I *WROTE* IT.
THE *OTHER* DIALOG, BEFORE WE CHANGED IT, *THAT* WAS BETTER.
YEAH, I *TOLD YOU* THAT YESTERDAY.
NEXT TIME, MAKE SURE I'M *LISTENING*.
ALL RIGHT, CHILDREN, WE BREAK UNTIL *TOMORROW MORNING*!
GET DRUNK, GET LAID, I *DO NOT* CARE... JUST BE *ON TIME*!
CITIZEN'S
ATIONAL BANK
SO, WHAT DO YOU WANNA *DO*?
GET THE *OLD PAGES* TO MISS SILVER...
WE'LL SHOOT HER *CLOSE-UP* AGAIN IN THE MORNING AND CHEAT THE LIGHT.
AND CHARLIE... I EXPECT *MORE* FROM TONIGHT'S REWRITES.

CHARLIE HAD BEEN LOOKING FORWARD TO THESE LOCATION SHOOTS.
A CHANCE TO GET AWAY FROM THE STUDIO LOT...
...WHERE HE'D BEEN ON THE VERGE OF LOSING IT THE PAST FEW DAYS.
JUMPY... PARANOID...
STAGE
CONSTANTLY SEEING HORN RIM GLASSES OUT OF THE CORNER OF HIS EYE...
...WAITING FOR THE NEXT BAD THING TO HAPPEN.
BUT NOW THAT THEY'RE HERE...
ALL HE CAN THINK ABOUT IS WHEN THEY SHOT THESE SAME SCENES THE FIRST TIME.

HE CAN RUN FROM HIS TROUBLES, BUT NOT FROM HIS GHOSTS...
I DON'T THINK WE'RE SUPPOSED TO GO THAT WAY, VAL.
IT'S A SHORTCUT, CHARLIE...
C'MON... OLD MAN KAMP DOESN'T HAVE WILD DOGS ON PATROL.
I WOULDN'T BE SO SURE.
ANYWAY, THEY TOLD US TO STEER CLEAR OF THE MAIN HOUSE...
AND DO YOU ALWAYS DO WHAT YOU'RE TOLD TO...?
CHRIST, THAT MUST BE NO FUN AT ALL...
DOTTIE WAS STILL WORKING THE TYLER GRAVES/MAYA SILVER ANGLE WITH THE PRESS.
CLOSER, TY... REALLY PLANT ONE ON HER...
ACT LIKE THE CAMERA ISN'T EVEN HERE...

THE STUDIO HAD BOUGHT TYLER A CUSTOM ROADSTER AS A WRAP GIFT AND SHE HAD MAYA PRESENT IT TO HIM...
...WHILE HER PHOTOGRAPHER SNAPPED SHOTS OF THE HAPPY COUPLE.
GOOD, YES... THAT'S MUCH BETTER.
HAPPY COUPLE... RIGHT.
DOTTIE WAS CHARLIE'S BEST BET TO FIND OUT WHO MR. HORN-RIM GLASSES WAS WITHOUT GETTING ANY DEEPER INTO THE MIRE...
DOTTIE KNEW EVERYONE.
THE TROUBLE WAS, SHE'D BEEN GIVING HIM THE SILENT TREATMENT SINCE THAT NIGHT AT CIRO'S.
HEY, MAYA...
I THINK YOU HAVE A VISITOR.

BOY, SHE'S NOT GETTING OVER WHATEVER IT IS I DID ANYTIME SOON, IS SHE?
WHAT?
SORRY, I WAS READING.
THESE NEW PAGES ARE TERRIFIC, CHARLIE.
OH, UH... THANKS.
SO WHAT WERE YOU SAYING...?
AHH, NOTHING... YOU DON'T NEED MY TROUBLES.
SPEAKING OF TROUBLE...
HOW'S IT GOING WITH TYLER?
YEAH. HE LOOKED A BIT... UNHAPPY BACK THERE...
HE'S A MOODY ONE, THAT'S FOR SURE.
BUT TODAY WAS DIFFERENT... LIKE HE COULD BARELY EVEN FAKE A SMILE.
JAIL
ACTORS... THEY'RE ALL CRAZY...

SO... HAVE YOU EVER BEEN UP THIS WAY BEFORE?
YEAH. I DANCED AT A FEW PARTIES AT THE BIG HOUSE.
IT WASN'T A LOT OF FUN.
A BUNCH OF US, ALL DOLLED-UP LIKE SHOWGIRLS...
PUTTING ON A PRIVATE SHOW FOR THE STUDIO'S SALES REPS...
...ALL OF THEM DRUNK OUT OF THEIR MINDS.
YEAH, THAT DOESN'T SOUND LIKE MUCH FUN...
THIS WHOLE PLACE JUST GIVES ME THE CREEPS NOW.
I'LL BE HAPPY WHEN WE'RE DONE HERE...
WELL, THIS IS ME.
YOU WANT TO HELP ME RUN LINES FOR A WHILE? KEEP ME COMPANY?
SADLY, I HAVE REWRITING TO DO.
YOU MAY HAVE NOTICED OUR DIRECTOR IS KIND OF A SLAVE-DRIVER.

WELL, IF YOU FINISH EARLY... I'M JUST THREE DOORS *DOWN.*
GOOD NIGHT, CHARLIE.
OH, AND DON'T WORRY ABOUT *DOTTIE.*
JUST BUY HER SOME FLOWERS AND SAY YOU'RE SORRY.
BUT I DON'T EVEN KNOW WHAT I'M *SORRY* FOR.
JUST SAY "*FOR EVERYTHING*" THEN.
THAT'LL WORK?
IT'LL WORK WITH *HER.*
OH... THANKS.
Y'KNOW... I THINK YOU'RE STARTING TO LIKE ME AFTER ALL, CHARLIE.
YOU'RE CERTAINLY MAKING IT HARD *NOT* TO.

SHE'S RIGHT, HE THINKS.
HE DOES LIKE HER...

...EVEN THOUGH HE KIND OF HATES HIMSELF FOR IT.

BUT THERE'S SOMETHING HIDING BEHIND HER SMILE.

SOMETHING BROKEN.

AND CHARLIE'S ALWAYS BEEN DRAWN TO THE BROKEN ONES...
JESUS, WAS THAT AN ANIMAL?
NO. IT SOUNDED LIKE SOMEONE WAS SCREAMING...

VAL? WHAT ARE YOU DOING?
LET'S GO SEE WHAT IT IS...
HEY, DAMN IT...
WAIT FOR ME...
VAL? HEY, DON'T GET TOO FAR...
SHHHHH... BE QUIET.
LISTEN... VOICES.
WE SHOULD GO BACK.
NO... I THINK I KNOW WHAT'S GOING ON...
I TOLD YOU... I PRACTICALLY GREW UP HERE.
DAMN IT.

JESUS...
HEY - HEY -- HELP ME...
BEFORE HE GETS BACK.
JESUS.
PLEASE... HURRY...
DO NOT UNTIE HER...
...SHE KNOWS EXACTLY WHAT SHE DID TO DESERVE THIS.
WHAT DID SHE DO?
MISTER KAMP?
GET OUT OF HERE, BOTH OF YOU...
THIS IS PRIVATE BUSINESS.
WHAT DID SHE DO?

HOW DARE YOU QUESTION ME.

UNTIE HER, CHARLIE.
VAL, THAT'S AL KAMP.

I KNOW WHO HE IS.
UNTIE HER.

DON'T YOU FUCKING TOUCH HER..

SLAAAP

...

YOU... I REMEMBER YOU...
OH, I DOUBT THAT.

NO... I REMEMBER. YOU WERE ALWAYS A STUCK-UP LITTLE BITCH...

...EVEN WHEN YOU WERE A KID.

I'M SORRY, SIR...

...BUT MISTER MASON SEEMS TO BE OUT AT THE MOMENT.
ARE YOU SURE?

YES SIR, HE DIDN'T ANSWER, SO I OPENED THE DOOR...
HIS LUGGAGE IS STILL HERE, BUT HE'S NOT.

FUCKING GIL, HE THINKS...
OKAY, CAN I LEAVE MY NUMBER FOR HIM?

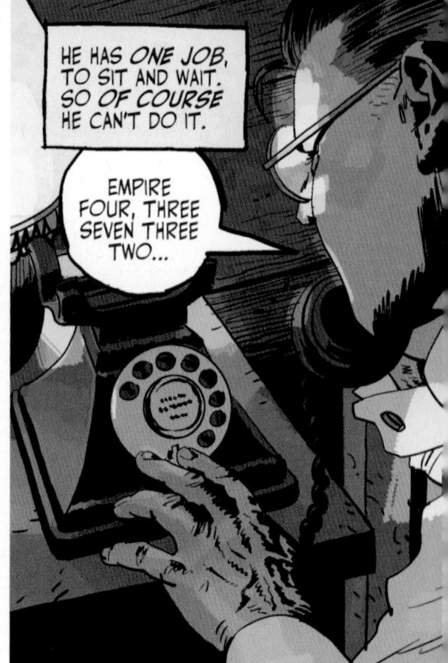
HE HAS ONE JOB, TO SIT AND WAIT. SO OF COURSE HE CAN'T DO IT.
EMPIRE FOUR, THREE SEVEN THREE TWO...

NO ONE CAN EVER DO WHAT THEY'RE SUPPOSED TO ANYMORE...

COME ON, GIL...
...WHERE THE HELL ARE YOU?

YOU WANNA KNOW WHAT I LOVE ABOUT GUYS LIKE YOU...?
YOU DON'T KNOW WHEN TO QUIT.
IT'S LIKE YOU ALL READ DON QUIXOTE TOO YOUNG TO REALIZE IT WAS A FUCKING JOKE.
BRICATION

YOU'RE LECTURING ME ABOUT DON QUIXOTE?
WHAT? I CAN'T READ A BOOK?
ANYWAY, MY POINT IS -- QUIXOTE'S THE ASSHOLE OF THE STORY.
HIS "NOBLE IDEALS" WERE ALREADY A JOKE THREE HUNDRED YEARS AGO.
BUT HERE WE ARE IN THE GODDAM 1940S...
AN' GUYS LIKE YOU STILL CAN'T LOOK AT THE WORLD AND SEE WHAT IT REALLY IS.
AND YOU THINK THAT'S A VIRTUE.
BUT TRUST ME... YOU ARE THE ASSHOLE OF YOUR STORY, GIL.

SCREW YOU.
KNOW WHY I CAME UP HERE IN THE FIRST PLACE?
WE GOT THIS ACTOR OUT AT THE RANCH SHOOTIN' A WESTERN...
"...AN' THIS GUY THINKS THE RULES DON'T APPLY TO HIM.
"MAYBE THAT'S NOT COMPLETELY HIS FAULT... THE STUDIO CODDLES THEM TOO MUCH..."
STILL, THIS GUY DOESN'T GET IT.
HOW GOOD HE HAS IT.
"NOW ME, I DON'T GIVE TWO SHITS WHO SCREWS WHO OR WHAT... SOME GUY WANTS TO FUCK OTHER GUYS...
"HELL... MORE POWER TO 'EM, I SAY."
BUT NOT EVERYONE'S LIKE ME...
AN' THIS ACTOR, HE JUST CAN'T BE DISCREET.
"THAT'S ALL I ASK OF THESE PEOPLE... JUST DON'T MAKE MY JOB ANY HARDER THAN IT NEEDS TO BE."

SO... NOW I HEAR HE'S FOOLIN' AROUND WITH ONE OF THE GODDAM EXTRAS...
LIKE HE DOESN'T EVEN GET HOW STUPID THAT IS.
"THIS NOBODY QUEER IS GONNA GO TO THE PRESS THE SECOND OUR GUY STOPS CALLIN' HIM. I'VE SEEN IT A HUNDRED TIMES..."
KAMP RANCH
THEN I'M STUCK PAYIN' OFF SOME SHITBIRD REPORTER...
AND NEXT MONTH WE START THE WHOLE MERRY-GO-ROUND OVER AGAIN.
"BUT YOU KNOW WHAT? THIS WAS THE STRAW THAT BROKE THIS PARTICULAR CAMEL'S BACK..."
I TRIED TO BE NICE, BUT THIS GUY'S LIKE THE DON QUIXOTE OF COCKSUCKING...
"SO I HAD TO REMIND HIM WHAT THE REAL WORLD FEELS LIKE."
COURSE I GOT A PROBLEM... THE KID'S A STAR.
I CAN'T TOUCH HIM.

SO, YOU KNOW WHAT I *DO*?
NO... WHAT?
"ME AN' MY GUYS MAKE A HOUSE CALL TO ***MISTER MOVIE STAR*** AND HIS BOY..."
AND I TAKE MY ***BRASS KNUCKLES*** TO THIS EXTRA'S ***FACE...***
"I BEAT THIS POOR KID UNTIL HE LOOKS MORE LIKE ***HAMBURGER*** THAN ANYTHING..."
...AN' THE WHOLE TIME I'M SAYIN' TO THIS *ACTOR* OF OURS...
"YOU DID THIS... YOU DID THIS..."
YOU BETTER ***BELIEVE*** HE GOT THE MESSAGE THIS TIME.
JESUS CHRIST...

THING IS, GIL... MOST OF THE TIME?
I'M JUST PROTECTIN' PEOPLE FROM THEMSELVES.
IF YOU'D LISTENED TO ME LAST YEAR, YOU'D STILL HAVE A CAREER.
SURE... AND NO SOUL.
LOOK -- WHAT DO YOU WANT, BRODSKY?
I DIDN'T EVEN TALK TO OLD MAN KAMP.
NO... YOU DIDN'T JUST NOT TALK TO HIM...
YOU DIDN'T SEE HIM, EITHER. GET ME?
THERE'S GONNA BE NO HEADLINES ABOUT MISTER KAMP LOSIN' HIS MARBLES.
YOU THINK I'D SQUEAL TO THE PRESS?
YOU WRECKED YOUR OWN LIFE FOR NOTHIN'. I DON'T KNOW WHAT YOU'LL DO.
SO IS THIS CONVERSATION GONNA BE ENOUGH...
...OR DO I HAVE TO GET THOSE BRASS KNUCKLES OUT AGAIN?

YEAH. THAT'S WHAT I FIGURED.
GOOD BOY, GIL.
IT'S THE WAY BRODSKY SAYS IT THAT'S THE PROBLEM.
LIKE EVERYTHING GIL EVER DID WAS JUST A FOOL PRETENDING NOT TO BE A COWARD.
AW DAMMIT... WHAT THE HELL...?
AND THAT'S JUST SOMETHING HE CAN'T ACCEPT.
HEY, PAL, RETIRED LAPD... WHAT'S THE HOLD-UP?
CAR WRECK. SOME MOVIE STAR DROVE RIGHT INTO THE EMBANKMENT.
HIGHWAY PATROL
NICE CAR, TOO... REAL SHAME.
AHH... SHIT...
AND THAT'S HOW GIL FINALLY MAKES A DECISION.
HE'S GOING TO BRING ALL THESE BASTARDS DOWN.
NO MATTER WHAT.

To Set the World on Fire

SCREW YOU, PAL.
CHARLIE AND GIL HADN'T BEEN GETTING ALONG THE PAST FEW DAYS... TO PUT IT MILDLY.

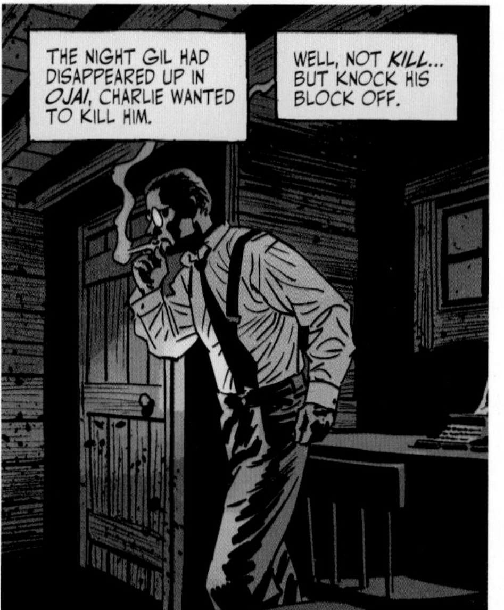
THE NIGHT GIL HAD DISAPPEARED UP IN OJAI, CHARLIE WANTED TO KILL HIM.
WELL, NOT KILL... BUT KNOCK HIS BLOCK OFF.

HE'D SAT UP STARING AT THE BLANK PAGE IN HIS TYPEWRITER...

...WITH HATRED.

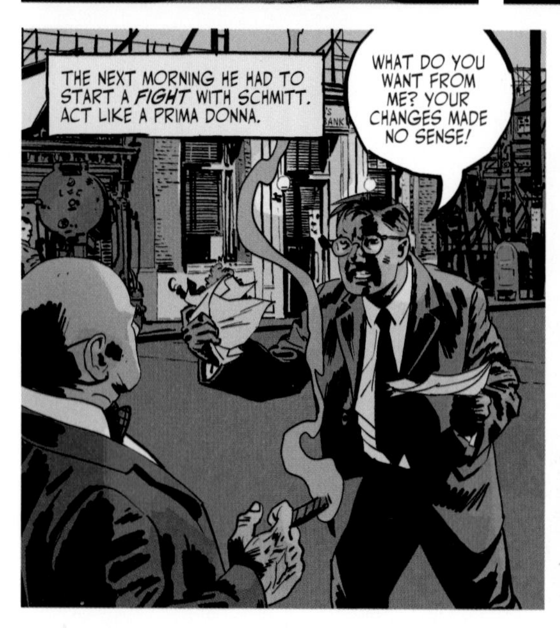
THE NEXT MORNING HE HAD TO START A FIGHT WITH SCHMITT. ACT LIKE A PRIMA DONNA.
WHAT DO YOU WANT FROM ME? YOUR CHANGES MADE NO SENSE!

IT WAS THE BEST COVER HE COULD COME UP WITH... EGO.
JUST RESHOOT THE ORIGINAL SCENE AGAIN.
STOP DRIVING ME CRAZY.

HE SHOULD'VE BEEN *FIRED*, BUT TYLER GRAVES HAD CRASHED HIS BRAND NEW *HOTROD* AND THE PRESS WAS DESCENDING...
SO THE STUDIO HAD ORDERED THEM TO WRAP *EARLY*, TO STAY OUT OF THE FRAY.
MOVIE STAR SMASH-UP
THERE WAS NO *TIME* FOR SCHMITT TO FIGHT.
YOU SON OF A BITCH...
STILL, THAT MINOR STROKE OF *LUCK* HADN'T MADE CHARLIE ANY *LESS* PISSED AT GIL...
BRODSKY WAS *ALL OVER ME!* WHAT WAS I *S'POSED* TO *DO?*
YOU WERE SUPPOSED TO KEEP YOUR *HEAD* DOWN! *THAT'S* WHAT!
AND EVEN AFTER THEY'D STOPPED YELLING, THE TENSION STAYED...
...HANGING THICK.
I SHOULD BE BACK AROUND *MIDNIGHT*.
JUST GO TO YOUR GODDAM *PREMIERE*...
I CAN TAKE MY OWN *DICTATION* FOR A CHANGE.

THE MOVIE PREMIERE HAD BEEN DOTTIE'S IDEA.
HE'D TAKEN MAYA'S ADVICE AND SENT HER SOME FLOWERS...

...BUT WHEN HE DROPPED BY TO APOLOGIZE IN PERSON, HE FOUND HER DEALING WITH HER OWN PROBLEMS.
ANYTHING I CAN DO TO HELP?
HUNH... YOU KNOW, MAYBE THERE *IS*...
PUBLICITY DEPT

MAYA'S WALKING THE RED CARPET AT BOGIE'S NEW PICTURE *TONIGHT*...
SHE DID A SONG IN THE *NIGHTCLUB* SCENE, I GUESS.

BUT WITH TY IN THE *HOSPITAL*, SHE DOESN'T HAVE A DATE.
YOU WANT ME TO...?

DON'T GET TOO *EXCITED*, MISTER...
YOU'D BE AN ESCORT, THAT'S ALL.

THE PRESS ARE GOING TO BE SWARMING THE JOINT...
...AND I CAN'T HAVE IT LOOK LIKE SHE'S STEPPING OUT ON PRINCE *CHARMING* WHILE HE'S IN TRACTION.

I NEED SOMEONE... *UNTHREATENING*...
THIS IS STARTING TO FEEL A LITTLE INSULTING.

I MEAN SOMEONE IT'S *OBVIOUS* IS JUST A *FRIEND*.
THINK YOU CAN *HANDLE* THAT?

NOT MAKING *MOON EYES* AT HER WHILE THE CAMERAS ARE FLASHING?
I WILL DO MY BEST, MA'AM.

OH CHRIST... I'M DOOMED.

SAY, UH, *DOTTIE*...
DO YOU KNOW A *PRODUCER* AROUND TOWN... HORN-RIM GLASSES, BLONDE CREW-CUT?

WHAT'S HIS *NAME*?
I DON'T KNOW, THAT'S WHY I'M ASKING.

THAT COULD BE *ANYONE*, CHARLIE.

WHAT'S THE HUBBUB WITH HIM?
AH, NOTHING...
JUST SAW HIM AT A PARTY, LOOKED LIKE SOMEONE I USED TO KNOW.
ALL RIGHT, KEEP YOUR SECRETS.
AND JUST LIKE THAT, HE FELT LIKE A HEEL AGAIN.
HE WANTED TO TELL DOTTIE EVERYTHING...
JUST LIKE HE WANTED TO TELL GIL HE THINKS HE'S REMEMBERED SOMEONE FROM THE NIGHT OF VAL'S MURDER.

BUT HE'S GOT A SICK FEELING IN HIS GUT ABOUT THIS GUY... AND UNTIL HE KNOWS WHO HE IS... MURDERER, FBI PLANT, OR JUST ANOTHER SUIT...
HE'S NOT TAKING ANY CHANCES.
HEY -- WOW... YOU LOOK STUNNING...
NOT LETTING ANYONE ELSE GET STUCK IN HIS MESS.
WHY, MISTER PARISH, WHERE HAVE YOU BEEN ALL MY LIFE?

THE PROBLEM IS, GIL'S ALREADY PLANNING A BRAND NEW MESS...
AND HE DOESN'T FEEL BAD FOR NOT TELLING CHARLIE.
THE WAY HE SEES IT, CHARLIE'S PART OF THE PROBLEM...
CHARLIE'S GIVEN UP.
DOESN'T WANT ANYTHING TO *DISRUPT* HIS LITTLE LIFE...
...JUST OUTSIDE THE SPOTLIGHT.
HEY GIL, GOOD TO SEE YA'...
HE'S IN THE BACK ROOM.
sed for
Private
Event
THANKS.

DASHIELL HAMMETT HAD ORGANIZED AN INFORMAL MEETING.
THE ORGANIZATION HE CHAIRED WAS RAISING MONEY TO HELP VICTIMS OF THE BLACKLIST.
...AND THEN OUR MAN ACTUALLY STEALS A *FERRIS WHEEL*, IF YOU CAN BELIEVE THAT.

GIL DIDN'T KNOW HAMMETT *WELL*... THEY'D GOTTEN SMASHED TOGETHER A FEW TIMES BACK IN THE OLD DAYS...
HANG ON, FELLAS... I'LL BE RIGHT BACK.

BUT HE KNEW HIM *WELL ENOUGH* TO KNOW MOST OF HIS FRIENDS DIDN'T CALL HIM *DASH*...
HEY SAM, THANKS FOR THE CALL...

HOW'VE YOU *BEEN*, GIL?
AH, YOU KNOW... THIS CRAZY FUCKING TOWN...

ARE YOU FINDING ANY WORK OUT THERE?
NOT ENOUGH, BUT... YEAH...

I WAS *REAL* SORRY TO SEE YOU GET SUCKED INTO THIS...

YOU DON'T DESERVE THIS CRAP, NONE OF YOU DO.
OH HELL, DON'T GET ME STARTED ON WHAT I DESERVE...
I'LL START THINKING I GOT OFF EASY.
WELL, I GUESS YOU COULD SAY THAT ABOUT ANY OF US.
SAY, ONE OF THE FELLAS HERE'S BEEN WRITING FOR THE COMICS...
CRIME DOESN'T PAY, SOME KID STUFF... SAYS THEY'RE LOOKING FOR WRITERS...
SURE, I'LL TALK TO HIM. I LIKED YOUR STRIP.
NO, THIS IS COMIC BOOKS, NOT IN THE NEWSPAPERS.
OH, OKAY... HEY, CAN I BUY YOU A DRINK AFTER THIS?
GOT SOMETHING I NEED SOME ADVICE ON.
SURE, WHAT IS IT?
OH, UH... IT'S NOT SOMETHING I CAN TALK ABOUT TOO MUCH, BUT...
...LET'S SAY I'M WORKING ON A MURDER STORY.

MAYA! OVER HERE!
MAYA! MAYA!
HEY!
HEY!
HEY, PAL -- GET OUTTA THE *SHOT*. YOU'RE IN-FRAME.
OH, SORRY...
CHARLIE NEVER FELT MORE *REMOVED* FROM HUMANITY THAN HE DID AT EVENTS LIKE THIS.
THE MOB OF SCREAMING VOICES... CRUSHING EACH OTHER FOR AN AUTOGRAPH...

OF COURSE, THEY'RE JUST THE MORE PRIMAL VERSION OF THE SAME DISEASE HE SUFFERS FROM.
HE KNOWS THAT.
CHARLIE'S JUST A *MOTH* WHO FIGURED OUT HOW TO GET CLOSER TO THE *FLAME*.
BUT *MAYA*, AND PEOPLE LIKE HER, THEY DID HIM ONE BETTER...
THEY FIGURED OUT HOW TO *BE* THE FLAME, INSTEAD.

OKAY... C'MON, ESCORT...
WE'RE GOING TO BE LATE TO THE AFTER PARTY...
OH... YOU ALL DONE WITH YOUR FANS?
FANS? THEY DON'T EVEN KNOW WHO I AM...
THEY JUST THINK THEY'RE SUPPOSED TO.
SHE'S SO GOOD AT THIS, CHARLIE THINKS.
WHY CAN'T HE BE MORE LIKE HER, ACTUALLY APPRECIATING THE MOMENT...
INSTEAD OF ALWAYS BEING CAUGHT UP IN THE PAST?

THAT'S *ALWAYS* BEEN HIS PROBLEM...
EVEN WHEN HE USED TO DREAM OF A FUTURE, TOO.
BUT NOW HE JUST DREAMS ABOUT *VAL*, EVEN WHEN HE'S AWAKE...
HIS MIND CONSTANTLY *DRIFTING* TO HER...
PULLING HIM FURTHER OUT TO SEA.
OH SHIT... *DESI ARNAZ* IS PLAYING.
MY... UM, MY *EX* IS IN HIS BAND.
YOU WANT TO LEAVE?
NO... IT'S FINE.
THIS IS THE *JOB*, RIGHT?
IF YOU SAY SO.

HE SEES THAT BROKEN LOOK CROSS HER FACE AGAIN, BEFORE IT DISAPPEARS BEHIND A NATURAL SMILE...
AS HER FEET AND HIPS START TO MOVE TO THE RHYTHM.
MAYBE SHE CAN DISTRACT HIM AFTER ALL, HE THINKS...
BUT THEN SHE MISSES A STEP... AND HE FOLLOWS HER EYES TO THE STAGE...
TO THE TRUMPET PLAYER.
WHO IS THAT?
YOU DON'T KNOW JACK JONES? FLAPJACK?
OH... YEAH, SURE... OF COURSE.
YOU OKAY?
IT'S NOTHING... JUST CURIOUS.
HE DIDN'T USED TO PLAY WITH DESI.

IT'S NOT NOTHING... BUT CHARLIE DOESN'T NOTICE.
HE'S ALREADY BEING PULLED BACK UNDER THE WAVES.
HE'D WRITTEN A DOZEN MURDER PICTURES, OR PARTS OF THEM, AT LEAST...
BUT ALL HE'D BEEN THINKING ABOUT THE PAST FEW WEEKS IS WHO COULD'VE MURDERED VAL...
HE'D FORGOTTEN TO ASK WHY.
BUT NOW HE'S REMEMBERING THAT NIGHT IN THE WOODS WITH OLD MAN KAMP...
AND HOW SHAKEN VAL WAS BY IT.
SHE SAID SHE'D PRACTICALLY GROWN UP ON THAT RANCH, AND HE KEPT WONDERING...
WHAT HAD SHE SEEN THERE?
HEY... JACK?
YOU IN THERE?

OH... HEY, CHARLIE. JUST HAVIN' A LITTLE DRINK.
COME ON BACK.
WHAT'S ON YOUR MIND, WRITER MAN?
WELL... I JUST...
I'VE BEEN THINKING ABOUT VAL...
IT JUST DOESN'T SIT RIGHT... HER KILLING HERSELF...
LIKE IT KEEPS GNAWING AT ME.
SHIT, MAN... I NEVER THOUGHT SHE'D GO THAT WAY, EITHER...
BUT YOU NEVER KNOW WHAT'S INSIDE ANYONE'S HEAD. NOT REALLY.
YEAH. I GUESS NOT...
CHARLIE THE HEEL, HE THINKS, AS HE LIES HIS WAY TO THE QUESTIONS HE REALLY CAME TO ASK...
THIS IS HOW THE PRIVATE EYE USUALLY DOES IT, RIGHT?
YOU KNOW, WE HAD A RUN-IN WITH OLD MAN KAMP JUST A FEW WEEKS BEFORE SHE DIED...
REALLY?
THOUGHT HE WAS LOCKED UP IN SOME HOSPITAL SOMEWHERE.

NO, HE'S JUST UP AT THE RANCH... OUT OF SIGHT.
ANYWAY, IT WAS... STRANGE. A LITTLE SCARY, EVEN.
THE OLD MAN REALLY GOT UNDER HER SKIN.
SHIT... I BET HE DID.
SHE SAID YOU ALL PRACTICALLY GREW UP ON THAT RANCH... IN THE KRAZY KIDS DAYS...
I KEEP THINKING MAYBE SOMETHING HAPPENED BACK THEN...
SOMETHING SHE COULDN'T LIVE WITH.
YOU THINKING YOU COULDA SAVED HER?
MAN, DIDN'T YOU LEARN ANYTHING IN THE WAR?
NO... NO, I GUESS NOT.

YOU KNOW, MOSTLY A T TIME...
ALL US KIDS RUNNING AROUND... PLAYIN'...
BUT YEAH...
SOME REAL FUCKED-UP SHIT WENT ON UP THERE SOMETIMES...
BEIN' RICH AIN'T ENOUGH FOR MOST RICH MEN.
THEY GOTTA ACT LIKE THE GODDAM EMPEROR OF ROME, TOO.
I GOT LUCKY. I NEVER HAD TO GO TO THOSE PARTIES.
BUT VAL WENT?
YOU KNOW WHAT?
THIS IS SOME DEPRESSING SHIT, CHARLIE.
DO ME A FAVOR, MAN... LET THE LADY REST IN PEACE.
SHE WANTED OUT. LET HER BE OUT.

CHARLIE WISHES IT WAS THAT SIMPLE...
BUT NOTHING IS ANYMORE.

HEY, I WAS LOOKING FOR YOU.
WHY DON'T WE GET OUT OF HERE?
YEAH... LET'S DO THAT.

YOU *OKAY*, MAYA?
I'M FINE... I'M JUST A TERRIBLE PERSON.

WELCOME TO THE *CLUB*.
ALWAYS ROOM FOR ONE MORE.

GIL AND CHARLIE HAD A RUNNING ARGUMENT ABOUT *LIQUOR* AND WHAT IT WAS GOOD FOR...
OF COURSE, THEY WERE CHRONIC DRUNKS. ALCOHOLICS WHO WERE JUST FINE WITH THAT DIAGNOSIS.
SO THIS WAS SOMETHING THEY THOUGHT ABOUT A LOT.
CHARLIE'S THEORY WAS THAT IT SHUT DOWN THE PART OF YOUR BRAIN THAT COULD TELL THE DIFFERENCE BETWEEN A GOOD IDEA...
... AND A *BAD* ONE.
IT MADE GENIUSES INTO *IDIOTS*.
CHARLIE ONLY REALLY VALUED LIQUOR FOR ITS *WORST* ASPECT.
THAT IT COULD WIPE YOUR MEMORY CLEAN... FOR A TIME, AT LEAST.

BUT GIL, HE THINKS LIQUOR JUST MAKES YOU MORE BOLD.
THAT WHEN YOU'RE PLASTERED, YOU SAY AND DO THE THINGS YOU REALLY WANT TO ALL THE TIME.
BECAUSE JUST LIKE WITH A GOOD JOKE...
CINESTAR
Why Did She Do It?
THE TRAGIC DEATH OF A STAR-TO-BE
THERE'S ALWAYS MORE TRUTH THAN LIES INSIDE A DRUNK.
WELL, LOOK, IF THIS WAS REAL LIFE...
... THEN I'D SAY YOUR DETECTIVE WOULD WANT TO STAY THE HELL AWAY FROM THE WHOLE MESS...
THERE ARE SOME PEOPLE YOU JUST DON'T WANT TO CROSS.

BUT THIS IS A STORY WE'RE TALKING ABOUT... RIGHT?
YEAH, OF COURSE...
SO... WHAT WOULD MY GUY DO TO TRY TO BUST IT OPEN?
TO EXPOSE THESE FAT-CATS?
IN THE PINKERTONS, SOMETIMES WE'D PROVOKE PEOPLE.
TRY TO GET THEM TO DO SOMETHING STUPID.
PEOPLE GET REAL STUPID REAL FAST WHEN THEY THINK YOU KNOW SOMETHING.
UH HUNH... YEAH...
RICH MEN ARE GREEDY, GIL... BUT THEIR REAL CURRENCY IS SECRETS.
I GUESS ONCE YOU'VE GOT ALL THE MONEY IN THE WORLD, THAT'S THE ONLY THING LEFT TO BARGAIN WITH.

BUT GIL, HE THINKS LIQUOR JUST MAKES YOU MORE BOLD.
THAT WHEN YOU'RE PLASTERED, YOU SAY AND DO THE THINGS YOU REALLY WANT TO ALL THE TIME.
BECAUSE JUST LIKE WITH A GOOD JOKE...
CINESTAR
Why Did She Do It?
THE TRAGIC DEATH OF A STAR-TO-BE
THERE'S ALWAYS MORE TRUTH THAN LIES INSIDE A DRUNK.
WELL, LOOK, IF THIS WAS REAL LIFE...
... THEN I'D SAY YOUR DETECTIVE WOULD WANT TO STAY THE HELL AWAY FROM THE WHOLE MESS...
THERE ARE SOME PEOPLE YOU JUST DON'T WANT TO CROSS.

BUT THIS IS A STORY WE'RE TALKING ABOUT... RIGHT?
YEAH, OF COURSE...
SO... WHAT WOULD MY GUY DO TO TRY TO BUST IT OPEN?
TO EXPOSE THESE FAT-CATS?
IN THE PINKERTONS, SOMETIMES WE'D PROVOKE PEOPLE.
TRY TO GET THEM TO DO SOMETHING STUPID.
PEOPLE GET REAL STUPID REAL FAST WHEN THEY THINK YOU KNOW SOMETHING.
UH HUNH... YEAH...
RICH MEN ARE GREEDY, GIL... BUT THEIR REAL CURRENCY IS SECRETS.
I GUESS ONCE YOU'VE GOT ALL THE MONEY IN THE WORLD, THAT'S THE ONLY THING LEFT TO BARGAIN WITH.

GIL...?
HEY GIL... WAKE UP.
... WHUU... HUNH...?
... SHIT... TIME IS IT...?
ALMOST SEVEN. YOU BETTER GET HOME...
...OR MELBA WILL HAVE OUR ASSES FOR BREAKFAST.
SEVEN...? YOU HAD A LONG NIGHT...
NAH... JUST FELL ASLEEP IN A BOOTH AT THE AFTER PARTY.
HOW'D THE WRITING GO?
OH... UM...
GOOD... IT WENT GOOD.

MORNIN' MISTER THURSBY...
MORNING, JEFFERSON.
SOMETHING THE MATTER, SIR?
NO, IT'S FINE.
BUT GO CALL BRODSKY FOR ME.
I KNOW WHAT REALLY HAPPENED
TELL HIM I NEED TO SEE HIM FIRST THING THIS MORNING.
HAPPENED

The Sound of Waves

BUT THEY THINK I'LL LOSE SOME VISION IN THIS EYE.
YOU GOT OFF LUCKY.
WHAT WERE YOU THINKING, TY?
THE POLICE TOLD US YOU WERE TRYING TO KILL YOURSELF.
I WASN'T...
IT WAS THAT GODDAM CAR.
LIKE I'M JUST SOME DUMB BITCH THEY CAN TREAT LIKE DIRT...
THEN GIVE ME SOMETHING PRETTY TO MAKE IT ALL OKAY.
SO WHAT, WAS THAT YOUR RESIGNATION LETTER?
CRASHING A CAR?
A BIT DRAMATIC, ISN'T IT?
WHAT IF IT WAS?
YOU ALREADY KNOW WHAT.
OR IS "MOVIE STAR RETIRES IN SHAME AFTER DRUNKEN CRASH" A HEADLINE YOU WANT TO SEE?

JESUS... I THOUGHT WE WERE FRIENDS, DOTTIE.
WE ARE. THAT'S WHY I'M TELLING YOU.
I NEVER SAID I WAS QUITTING.
BUT YOU HAVE TO KEEP THAT ANIMAL BRODSKY AWAY FROM ME.
I DON'T CARE HOW MUCH TROUBLE I'M IN... I'M NOT TALKING TO THAT BASTARD.
IT'S OKAY... I'LL TELL EVERYONE I'M HANDLING YOU, PERSONALLY.
I WOULDN'T WORRY ABOUT BRODSKY, ANYWAY...
HE'S BEEN OFF ON SOME SECRET JOB FOR THE BOSS MAN ALL WEEK.
IT'S VERY HUSH-HUSH... BUT YOU KNOW ME...
I'VE GOT EYES EVERYWHERE.

IT'S SO PEACEFUL HERE...
... I LOVE IT.
YEAH. IT'S NICE...
HEY, DID I HEAR THE PHONE A MINUTE AGO?
YES. IT WAS DOTTIE.
REALLY... HOW'D SHE FIND YOU?
I LEFT THIS NUMBER WITH THE ANSWERING SERVICE.
THAT WASN'T SUCH A GREAT IDEA...
WHAT DID SHE WANT?
NOTHING, REALLY.
I MIGHT HAVE TO GO STAND NEXT TO TY WHEN HE TALKS TO THE PRESS ABOUT HIS ACCIDENT.

TODAY?
MAYBE. SHE'S NOT SURE HE'S *READY* FOR IT YET...
... BUT SHE'S GONNA CALL BACK LATER.
SO WE MIGHT HAVE TO GO HOME EARLY?
ONLY IF SHE CALLS.
WHAT IF I RIP THE *PHONE* OUT OF THE WALL?
YOU'RE *TERRIBLE*.
ME? YOU'RE THE ONE GIVING OUT THE *NUMBER* TO OUR SECRET HIDEAWAY...
C'MERE, YOU!
HEY -- !

STOP - STOP IT -- *HA HA!*
YOU'RE CRAZY!

CHARLIE KNEW THE WEEKEND WOULDN'T LAST... BUT CUTTING IT SHORT...
THAT WOULDN'T BE EASY.

HE AND MAYA HAD BEEN TRADING PRIVATE GLANCES ON THE LOT ALL WEEK...

EVER SINCE THE NIGHT OF HER MOVIE PREMIERE.

BUT THEY'D ONLY MANAGED ONE QUICK MOMENT ALONE.

AND HE'D USED IT TO MAKE A PLAN...
A WEEKEND OUT OF TOWN.

A LITTLE PLACE HE KNEW, JUST UP THE ROAD FROM MALIBU.

SAND AND SURF. THE SOUND OF THE WAVES ALL DAY AND NIGHT.
THEY HAD FOOD AND BOOZE DELIVERED IN, AND TRIED NOT TO LEAVE THE BEDROOM AT ALL.
THAT WAS THE PLAN...
REMAIN NOT-SO-MILDLY DRUNK AND GET A BIT CRAZY.
HER SMILING EYES WERE LIKE A CONSTANT CHALLENGE...
LIKE THEY WERE SAYING "DO WE EVEN NEED TO SLEEP?"

CHARLIE HAD ALWAYS BEEN A SUCKER FOR THIS PART... THE FIRST DAYS.
THE DAYS WHEN YOU LET YOURSELF BELIEVE THE LIES...
NOT JUST THAT THERE'S SOMEONE WHO TRULY SEES YOU...
TRULY UNDERSTANDS YOU... TO YOUR SOUL...
... BUT THAT YOU EVEN WANT THEM TO.
THAT'S THE SWEETEST LIE, THE ONE YOU TELL YOURSELF.

SATURDAY NIGHT SHE COOKED THEM DINNER, AND AFTERWARD CHARLIE PUT ON THE RADIO...

GLENN MILLER... LENA HORNE... THE ANDREWS SISTERS...

THEY LAUGHED AND DANCED...

UNTIL HE COULDN'T STAND IT ANYMORE...

JUST HOLDING HER.
RIIPPP

WHAT IS THAT, THAT HAPPENS TO YOU WHEN YOU DANCE?
WHAT DO YOU MEAN?

IT'S HARD TO DESCRIBE...
LIKE SOME SECRET LIGHT GOES ON BEHIND YOUR EYES.

LIKE YOU'RE SOMEWHERE ELSE.
I GUESS THAT'S TRUE...

IT'S WHAT I WAS BORN FOR, DANCING.
MY PAPA WAS A MUSICIAN...

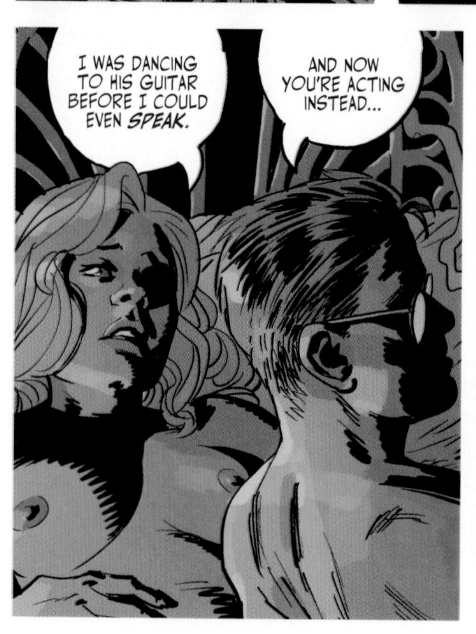
I WAS DANCING TO HIS GUITAR BEFORE I COULD EVEN SPEAK.
AND NOW YOU'RE ACTING INSTEAD...

SURE. IT WAS THE NATURAL NEXT STEP.
THAT SOUNDS LIKE ONE OF DOTTIE'S SCRIPTED ANSWERS.

HEH... I GUESS IT IS...
BUT IT'S TRUE...

I LOVE DANCING...
I LOVE WHO I *AM* WHEN I'M DANCING...
BUT CAN YOU NAME *ANY* WOMEN DANCERS BESIDES GINGER ROGERS AND CYD CHARISSE?
ALL THOSE FACELESS GIRLS... LITTLE WIND-UP DOLLS DANCING IN A ROW.
THERE ARE MOMENTS IN LIFE THAT ARE LIKE A PERFECT SONG...
THE KIND THAT REALLY GETS INSIDE YOU.

LIKE THE MOMENT MAYA MENTIONED HER FATHER...
WHEN SHE ALMOST LET SOME SORROW SHOW THROUGH.

CHARLIE HAD NEVER WRITTEN *ANYTHING* THAT ELEGANT... EVEN WHEN HE COULD STILL WRITE.

BUT HE'D ALWAYS ENVIED SONGWRITERS. TO HIM, THEY WERE LIKE ALCHEMISTS...
PULLING EMOTION AND MEMORY OUT OF THIN AIR.

TRANSPORTING YOU.

MAYA WAS LIKE A SONG...
HIS DRUNKEN EYES SAW THAT NOW.

A STRANGE, HAUNTED MELODY...

SO... NOT THAT I'M COMPLAINING, BUT WHAT'S WITH THE CLEAN-SHAVEN LOOK?
I'VE NEVER BEEN WITH ANY GIRLS THAT DID THAT.
SO MANY QUESTIONS, CHARLIE...

WHY DON'T WE TALK ABOUT YOU FOR A CHANGE?
ME? I'M NOBODY.
C'MON... WHY'D YOU DO IT? IS IT A DANCER THING?
NO...
IT'S A FUNNY STORY, ACTUALLY...
...BUT YOU CAN'T REPEAT IT...
AND IT DOES SEEM FUNNY, AT FIRST.
HOW HER AGENT, GREAVEY, INSISTED SHE SHAVE HERSELF DOWN THERE BEFORE THE SCREEN TEST.
AND HOW OLD MAN THURSBY MADE HER STRIP FOR HIM, BUT THEN RECOILED WHEN SHE OPENED HER ROBE.

HE TOLD HER SHE LOOKED LIKE A *CHILD*, HIS OLD MAN VOICE TREMBLING...
LIKE HE WAS EXCITED, BUT ASHAMED AT THE SAME TIME...
A LOT OF MEN ARE LIKE THAT IN HER EXPERIENCE, SHE SAYS.
AND SHE'S LAUGHING ABOUT IT, BUT BY THAT POINT CHARLIE ISN'T SO AMUSED ANYMORE.

WHAT'S *WRONG*, CHARLIE?

YOU KNOW WHAT'S WRONG.

I DID WHAT I ALWAYS DO...
TRIED TO DISTRACT MYSELF, SO I COULD JUST FORGET...

BUT THAT DOESN'T WORK, DOES IT?
I SHOULD KNOW BETTER, AFTER GERMANY...

I'M SORRY, VAL...

I'M SORRY...

SO, WE BETTER GET ON THE ROAD...
YOU READY?
I GUESS SO... READY AS I'LL EVER BE.

MAYA DROPPED CHARLIE OFF AT A BAR WHILE SHE WENT TO THE HOSPITAL FOR DOTTIE'S PRESS EVENT.
Formosa
SHE WAS GOING TO PICK HIM UP LATER, SO THEY'D HAVE A FEW MORE HOURS BEFORE THEY HAD TO GO BACK TO REAL LIFE.
BUT CHARLIE'S ALREADY GONE TO A DARKER PLACE...
HIS MIND CIRCLING DEAD GIRLS, AND THE INNOCENT KIDS THEY ONCE MUST HAVE BEEN.
WELL, IF IT ISN'T CAPTAIN BACKSTABBER HIMSELF...
...COLONEL GODDAM SHITHEEL, RIGHT HERE IN THE FLESH...
WHAT? SO I'M IN THE ARMY AND THE NAVY... ?
PICK ONE, FATHEAD.

LINCOLN KESSLER WAS AN OLD DRINKING BUDDY OF GIL'S.
SCREW *YOU*, PARISH. YOU'RE A FUCKING *COWARD*.
THIS WAS THE LAST THING CHARLIE NEEDED...
GIL MASON TAUGHT YOU EVERYTHING YOU KNOW...
SOME FUCKING ASSHOLE WHO DOESN'T KNOW THE REAL STORY.
AND YOU JUST GAVE HIM UP.
BACK OFF, LINC...
SOME FUCKING ASSHOLE ON HIS FUCKING HIGH HORSE...
YOU PICKED THE WRONG NIGHT TO GROW A SPINE.
OH, YOU'RE A TOUGH GUY NOW?
SPARE ME.
NOT TOUGH, BUT I'LL KNOCK *YOUR* TEETH OUT...
YOU *TALENTLESS* HACK.

OH YEAH, I'M SHIVERING IN MY SHOES HERE... I'M TERRIFIED.
I'M NOT WARNING YOU AGAIN.
Y'KNOW... GUYS LIKE YOU MAKE ME WANNA PUKE.
THE MAN WAS YOUR FRIEND, YOU SON OF A BITCH...
WHY DON'T YOU JUST GO FUCK HIS WIFE, TOO?
FUUCK YOU!
YOU THINK YOU KNOW ME?!
FUCKER!!

THINK I HAVEN'T DONE *WORSE* THAN *THAT*?!
SUCKER-*PUNCHING* MOTHERFUCKER...

YOU DON'T KNOW ME!

I'LL FUCKING KILL YOU!

I'LL KILL EVERY **FUCKING** ONE OF YOU!

FUU--

...FUHH...
YOU SHOULD REALLY LEARN HOW TO *FIGHT* SOMEDAY.

AHH... THERE'D BE NO *CHALLENGE* IF I KNEW WHAT I WAS DOING...
TRUE, BUT IT MIGHT SAVE YOU ON GLASSES REPAIR.
THESE ARE STILL USABLE... JUST A BIT...

...CRACKED.
HOLY SHIT.

THAT GUY.
FROM THE NIGHT VAL WAS KILLED.
I THINK WE'VE *MET*... CHARLIE PARISH, RIGHT?

YEAH...
DRAKE MILLER... I'M A PRODUCER ON THE LOT.
VICTORY STREET, I MEAN.

Y'KNOW, I'M A BIG FAN.
"AT THE END" IS STILL ONE OF MY FAVORITE PICTURES.

WHAT THE HELL IS HAPPENING HERE?
OH, THANKS...
SHAME YOU HAD TO GO UP AGAINST "CITIZEN KANE" AT THE OSCARS...
OTHERWISE YOU'D HAVE HAD IT IN THE BAG.
THAT WAS A LONG TIME AGO.
TRUE... IT WAS.

STILL, I'VE KEPT AN EYE ON YOU, CHARLIE...

YOUR WORK, I MEAN.

AND YOUR RECENT STUFF, IT'S JUST *NOT* THE SAME.
SOMETIMES IT DOESN'T EVEN SOUND LIKE *YOUR WRITING* AT ALL.
...UH... PEOPLE CHANGE, I GUESS...
SERIOUSLY... WHAT THE HELL *IS* THIS?
WHOA, PAL... MAYBE YOU BETTER SIT DOWN...
I'M FINE.
NONSENSE. YOU'RE STILL WOOZY... SIT.
LOOK, HERE'S MY CARD...
CALL ME AND MY GIRL'LL SET UP A LUNCH...
I THINK WE PROBABLY HAVE *A LOT* TO TALK ABOUT...
WHAT THE HELL IS

SHIT.
...?
SHIT SHIT SHIT...
WELL, THANK THE GODS... HE'S *ARRIVED*.
I WAS STARTING TO THINK YOU WERE STANDING ME UP, CHARLIE.
SORRY, I HAD A MINOR COMPLICATION.
OH MY GOD -- *CHARLIE!*
I KNOW, SORRY.
ARE YOU ALL RIGHT?
WHAT *HAPPENED*?
JUST BEING AN IDIOT...
IT *LOOKS* WORSE THAN IT IS.

OKAY... LET'S GET YOU BACK TO MY PLACE.
I'VE GOT A GOOD FIRST AID KIT.
CHARLIE NODS ALONG...
MY EX-HUSBAND USED TO COME HOME LIKE THIS ALL THE TIME.
BUT HE'S BUSY PONDERING THE *THREAT* BEHIND DRAKE MILLER'S WORDS.
BUT HE WAS A *MUSICIAN*...
WHO THE HELL *WAS* THAT GUY?
I MEAN, HE WAS ONE OF THE *CRAZY* ONES.
BUT YOU'RE A *WRITER*, CHARLIE.
...?
WRITERS ARE SUPPOSED TO BE *BORING*...
Call me. We need to talk - Tina
DON'T YOU KNOW THAT?

A Dead Giveaway

BRODSKY WAS GETTING TOO OLD FOR THIS CHICKENSHIT BULLSHIT.
ROOSEVELT HOTEL
AND THIS ONE WAS DEFINITELY THAT, *BULLSHIT*.

YET HERE HE WAS, IN THE LOBBY OF THE ROOSEVELT...
ON HALLO-FUCKING-WEEN...

STAKING OUT A *PACKAGE* HE KNEW DAMN WELL NO ONE WAS GOING TO SHOW UP FOR.

ALL BECAUSE THE OLD MAN HAD GOTTEN A *SECOND* NOTE...
'NOTHER GIN, BUDDY.
SURE THING.

THIS TIME IN THE MAIL, AND WITH A *RANSOM* DEMAND.
A *THOUSAND BUCKS*? THAT'S *IT*?
YES, TO BE LEFT BEHIND A *FICHUS* IN THE LOBBY...

I THOUGHT YOU WERE *HANDLING* THIS SITUATION, PHIL?

I'M STILL WORKING ON IT.
BUT THIS *ISN'T* ON THE UP-AND-UP, BOSS.

ALL WE'VE HAD FROM THIS GUY IS A THREAT... NO DETAILS.
AN' NOW HE'S ONLY ASKIN' FOR A *GRAND*?

THIS WHOLE THING JUST STINKS...
ALL THE SAME, IT'S STILL A THREAT.
SO YOU FIND WHOEVER'S SENDING THESE LITTLE NOTES...
AND YOU GET THE GODDAM DETAILS.
YOU FIND OUT WHAT THEY KNOW.
WHAT THEY KNOW IS BUPKIS...
BECAUSE PEOPLE WHO KNOW THINGS ASK FOR MORE MONEY.
NO... THIS IS SOMEONE FUCKING WITH HIM.
SOMEONE WHO KNOWS HE'LL HAVE TO EYEBALL EVERY COSTUMED PRICK WALKING BY...
SOME FUCKING JOKER.

TRICK OR TREAT!
TRICK OR TREAT!
WHY, JUST LOOK AT YOU TWO... WHAT LITTLE DARLINGS...
I'M A PIRATE!
WELL, HOW DOES A PIRATE FEEL ABOUT A BUTTERFINGER BAR?
IT'S REALLY NICE YOU COULD COME OUT...
THE KIDS HAVE MISSED SEEING THEIR UNCLE CHARLIE.
YEAH. IT'S GREAT TO SEE THEM HAVING SO MUCH FUN.
AND I HAVEN'T SEEN GIL THIS HAPPY IN...
SHIT... YOU TELL ME, I GUESS.
ARE YOU TWO STILL FIGHTING OR SOMETHING?

WHO CAN TELL MOST DAYS?
WHY?
BECAUSE GIL'S BEEN ALL SMILES THE PAST WEEK...
I ASSUMED YOU TWO HAD SOME KIND OF BREAKTHROUGH ON THE REWRITES.
I'VE, UH... I'VE MOSTLY BEEN LEAVING HIM TO HANDLE THE NOTES.
THE PAST FEW WEEKS HAVE BEEN, UM... BUSY.
OOH... I SEE. A NEW WOMAN IN THE PICTURE.
IS THAT WHY YOU'VE BEEN STARING OFF INTO SPACE?
OH UH, YEAH... YEAH, I GUESS. MAYBE.
THAT'S A LIE.
HE HAD BEEN THINKING ABOUT A WOMAN, BUT NOT MAYA.
NO, HE'D SPENT THE LAST THREE DAYS TRYING TO FIGURE OUT WHO ON GOD'S GREEN EARTH TINA WAS.
l me. We
d to talk
- Tina

WHY HAD DRAKE MILLER GIVEN HIM THIS NOTE INSTEAD OF HIS CARD?
HE'D THOUGHT THE GUY WAS TRYING TO INTIMIDATE HIM...
BUT NOW HE DIDN'T KNOW.
SO, WHO'S THE UNLUCKY LADY?
I'LL TELL YOU IF IT GETS SERIOUS.
THEN I'LL NEVER HEAR ABOUT HER.
NO DEAL, MISTER... TALK.
NAME, RANK, AND SERIAL NUMBER...
THAT'S ALL YOU'LL GET OUTTA ME.
DICK.
YOU KISS YOUR CHILDREN WITH THAT MOUTH?
GOD, NO...
HAVE YOU SEEN HOW FILTHY MY CHILDREN USUALLY ARE?

AHH, MELBA... GIL NEVER DESERVED HER, EVEN BEFORE HE SET THEIR LIVES ON FIRE.
STILL, CHARLIE SMILES AT THE SIGHT OF THEM ALL TOGETHER.
AND HIS MIND LINGERS FOR A MOMENT OR TWO ON THE MONTHS HE LIVED WITH THEM...
AFTER HE CAME HOME, ALL BROKEN.
RIGHT... AN' YOU KNOW WHAT STAGE IT'S AT?
YEAH, SURE.

EVERY YEAR, VICTORY STREET THREW A BIG HALLOWEEN PARTY.
IT WAS MR THURSBY'S FAVORITE HOLIDAY...
AND EVEN THOUGH HE'D STOPPED ATTENDING THE PARTY LONG AGO...
MOST EVERYONE ELSE ON THE LOT MADE AN APPEARANCE.
HEY, MORTY...
NO, IT'S CHARLIE.
CHARLIE WAS SUPPOSED TO MEET MAYA THERE...
FUNNY. GOOD ONE.
?
BUT HE WAS HOPING TO RUN INTO HIS NEW FRIEND WITH THE HORN-RIMMED GLASSES FIRST.
WELL, LOOK WHO WENT TO SOME EFFORT THIS YEAR...
I'M IMPRESSED, CHARLIE.
PEOPLE KEEP THINKING I'M MORTY.

YOU EVER PLANNING TO GET THOSE FIXED?
NAH... THE *GLASSES* ARE A DEAD GIVEAWAY.
I'LL GET AROUND TO IT.
SURE YOU WILL...
SO, YOU THINK SCHMITT'S GOING TO HIT THE *WRAP DATE* ON YOUR PICTURE?
IS THERE *ANOTHER* OPTION?
YES... THE OLD MAN COULD *FIRE* ALL OF YOU.

THEN I THINK WE'RE GONNA HIT OUR DATE.

WHO ARE YOU *LOOKING* FOR?

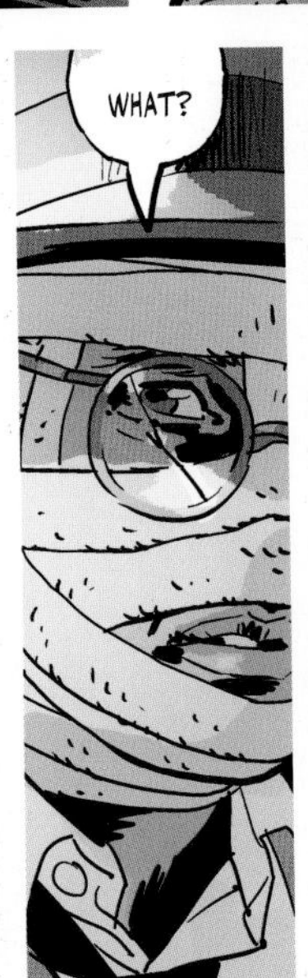

WHAT?

YOU KEEP LOOKING RIGHT *PAST ME*, OVER MY SHOULDER...

SORRY, JUST NOTICING ALL THE FANCY GET-UPS, I GUESS.
GOD... WERE YOU ALWAYS THIS BAD A LIAR?
WELL, I HAVEN'T SEEN MAYA YET, EITHER...
BUT PLEASE TELL ME YOU HAVEN'T FALLEN FOR HER.
YOU KNOW HOW STUPID THAT WOULD BE, RIGHT?
DOTTIE, I SWEAR - I'M NOT LOOKING FOR MAYA.
I MEAN IT. THEY HAVE BIG PLANS FOR THAT GIRL...
YOU'LL BE GROUND-UP LIKE HAMBURGER AND LEFT IN HER WAKE.
OKAY, RELAX... WARNING RECEIVED.
TRUST ME, CHARLIE, YOU DON'T WANT THAT ONE ANYWAY...
IT'S THE WAY SHE SAYS IT...
GIVES HIM A SUDDEN URGE TO TELL HER WHO HE'S REALLY LOOKING FOR, JUST TO PROVE HER WRONG.
BUT THAT WOULD BE A BAD IDEA...
I NEED ANOTHER DRINK... I'LL SEE'YA, DOT.

...AND HE'S ALREADY SURROUNDED BY A SEA OF BAD IDEAS.
LIKE TRYING TO FIND SOMEONE HE ONLY VAGUELY REMEMBERS AT A COSTUME PARTY.
BRILLIANT PLAN, CHARLIE.
GIRLS, THIS IS MY GOOD FRIEND *CHUCK*.
LADIES.
NICE COSTUME, WE SHOULD'VE CAST *YOU* INSTEAD OF MORTY.
YEAH, RIGHT...
HEY, EARL, YOU KNOW A PRODUCER ON THE LOT NAMED DRAKE MILLER?
DOESN'T RING A BELL, BUT ALL THOSE PINHEADS BLUR TOGETHER IN MY MIND...
WHY? HE OFFERING YOU A SCRIPT ON SOMETHING *GOOD*?
UH... COULD BE, *MAYBE*...
WELL, LET ME KNOW IF IT'S A GOOD ONE FOR *ME*, TOO...

NOW IF YOU'LL EXCUSE US, I'VE GOT A SWORD-SWALLOWING CONTEST TO JUDGE...
OF COURSE YOU DO.
UNLESS YOU WANT TO JOIN US?
GIRLS? ROOM FOR ONE MORE?
WHAT DOES HE DO?
I'M A WRITER.
EWW... NO.
SORRY CHUCK.
KIDS TODAY. NO RESPECT FOR REAL ARTISTS.

FUCKIN' EARL...
HE'D HAVE HAD BETTER LUCK ASKING HIM ABOUT THE MYSTERIOUS TINA, PROBABLY.
HEY, MORTY...

...GOD DAMN IT...
AND THEN CHARLIE HAS ONE OF THOSE MOMENTS...
THE KIND THAT LIFE JUST GIVES YOU SOMETIMES...
AND SUDDENLY HE REMEMBERS EXACTLY WHO TINA IS.
WHAT THE HECK, CHARLIE? I SAID IT WAS IMPORTANT.
THE GIRL FROM EARL'S PARTY... THE DANCER...
OR WAS SHE A SINGER?
SORRY, SORRY... THINK I LOST YOUR NUMBER.
WELL, C'MON... WE SHOULDN'T TALK HERE...
THAT PRICK BRODSKY MIGHT BE HIDING UNDER ONE OF THOSE MASKS.
BRODSKY?

HE WAS WAITING WHEN I GOT OUT OF REHEARSAL...
DRAGGED ME OFF TO SOME EMPTY DRESSING ROOM.
I THOUGHT IT WAS GOING TO BE THE USUAL ROUTINE THESE GUYS PULL...

BUT NO... HE JUST STARTS GIVING ME THE THIRD DEGREE...

... ABOUT THE NIGHT VALERIA SOMMERS KILLED HERSELF.

BRODSKY WAS ASKING ABOUT VAL?
YEAH, HE KNEW THAT I LEFT THE PARTY WITH HER THAT NIGHT...

AND HE WANTED TO KNOW WHO WAS WITH US.
BUT THERE WAS SOMETHING ELSE GOING ON...

WHAT DO YOU MEAN?
I MEAN HE SCARED THE SHIT OUT OF ME, CHARLIE.

"HE ASKED IF I WAS SMART ENOUGH TO KNOW NOT TO BE STUPID....
"THEN HE TOLD ME WHAT HAPPENED TO STUPID GIRLS... IN CASE I NEEDED A REMINDER."

JESUS...
YEAH, I KNOW... BUT I LIED TO HIM, ANYWAY.
I DIDN'T TELL HIM ABOUT YOU BEING WITH US...

BUT ONE OF THE OTHERS IS BOUND TO, SO YOU NEED TO WATCH YOUR BACK...
HE'S AFTER SOMETHING.

WHY WOULD YOU LIE FOR ME?
BECAUSE YOU'RE A NICE GUY...

AND I'M LEAVING, ANYWAY.
MY COUSIN GOT ME A GIG IN ATLANTIC CITY...

IT WAS NEVER GOING TO HAPPEN FOR ME HERE.

LISTEN, TINA... I'M ACTUALLY A BIT FOGGY ON THAT NIGHT...
WHO ELSE DID WE LEAVE WITH...?
IT WAS YOUR MOVIE STAR FRIEND, AND SOME PRODUCER...
AND SOME OTHER GUY I DIDN'T KNOW.

MOVIE STAR FRIEND?
EARL?

GOD, WHY AM I SURPRISED YOU DON'T REMEMBER ANY OF THIS?
I MEAN, YOU WERE SO DRUNK WHEN I SAW YOU AT THE FORMOSA...
WAIT -- YOU WERE AT THE FORMOSA?

YES, I SLIPPED YOU THAT NOTE WHEN MY DATE WASN'T LOOKING...
WE EVEN JOKED ABOUT IT.

HUH...

Y'KNOW, CHARLIE... MAYBE YOU SHOULD THINK ABOUT GETTING OUT OF THIS PLACE, TOO...

TINA LEAVES CHARLIE WITH MORE *QUESTIONS* THAN HE STARTED WITH...
AND THE ONE ANSWER SHE DOES HAVE, HE DOESN'T WANT TO BELIEVE...
EARL LEFT HIS OWN PARTY WITH THEM?
WHY HADN'T HE EVER *MENTIONED* IT?
THEY'D *TALKED* ABOUT THAT NIGHT... ABOUT VAL'S DEATH...
CHRIST, COULD *EARL*...?
NO. IT'S NOT POSSIBLE.
THE MAN HAD THE BEST LIFE IN THE WORLD, WHY WOULD HE -
THERE YOU ARE... *THANK GOD*.
MAYA -- HEY, WHERE'S YOUR COSTUME?

I'M NOT HERE FOR THE PARTY... I NEED HELP.
WHAT'S WRONG?
CAN YOU JUST... NOT ASK QUESTIONS, CHARLIE?
JUST COME WITH ME...
SHE'S TAKING A BIG RISK HERE, MAYA THINKS.
NEEDING PEOPLE IS ALWAYS A RISK.
NEEDING THEIR HELP IS EVEN WORSE...
16
BECAUSE THEN THEY GET CLOSE TO YOU...

CLOSE ENOUGH TO GUESS WHO YOU REALLY MIGHT *BE*, BEHIND THAT PLATINUM SMILE.
IT'S THE ONE ON THE CORNER...
25

LOOKS ABANDONED.
IT IS...

THERE'S NOTHING BUT *DOPE FIENDS* AND RATS IN THERE NOW.

MAYA, WHAT ARE WE *DOING*?

LOOKING FOR MY *EX-HUSBAND*...
I PROMISED HIS *MOTHER* I'D BRING HIM HOME TO HER.

ARE YOU *OKAY* WITH THAT?

YEAH... I'M FINE.

JUST STAY CLOSE TO ME IN HERE...
CHARLIE HAD SEEN SHOOTING GALLERIES BEFORE.
BACK IN KANSAS CITY, THE MOB RAN SMACK IN BACKROOMS ALL OVER THE GARMENT DISTRICT.
HIS FATHER HAD SPENT MOST OF THE DEPRESSION SLOWLY KILLING HIMSELF IN ONE OF THEM.
SO HE KNEW WHAT TO EXPECT.
WAIT -
HIS SURPRISE WAS THAT MAYA DID, TOO.
HERE... SHIT.
WAKE UP, MANDO... COME ON...
WELL, HIS FIRST SURPRISE...
EHH... QUÉ CARAJO...?

LET'S GET HIM UP.
I'VE GOT IT...
C'MON... USE YOUR **LEGS,** BUDDY...
...CHUPA MI VERGA...
JUST SHUT UP AND **WALK,** MANDO.

GO AHEAD, CHARLIE... **SPEAK.**

NO, IT'S JUST...
HE'S **MEXICAN.**

I WASN'T EXPECTING THAT...
WHY **WOULD** YOU BE?

THIS IS THE GUY YOU SAID PLAYS WITH *DESI ARNAZ*?
HE USED TO...
WHEN I MET HIM HE WAS IN MY *FATHER'S* BAND.
ONE OF THE BEST *TRUMPETERS* YOU'VE EVER HEARD...

AND NOW HIS MOUTH IS *SO BROKEN* HE COULDN'T EVEN WHISTLE.

WHAT HAPPENED TO HIM?
STUDIO SECURITY. THAT MAN -- *BRODSKY*?

MANDO JUST WOULDN'T QUIT COMING AROUND...

HE WAS GOING TO RUIN *EVERYTHING*.

MAYA DROPS CHARLIE A FEW BLOCKS FROM HIS APARTMENT...
AND HIS MIND SPINS AS HE WALKS HOME IN THE NIGHT AIR.

BRODSKY WRECKED THAT POOR BASTARD'S *WHOLE LIFE*...
AND FOR WHAT? THE STANDARD *JEALOUS EX* ROUTINE?

HE HATES HIMSELF FOR IT, BUT HIS MIND GOES BACK TO EARL.

IF - *SOMEHOW* - EARL WAS VAL'S KILLER...
...SHIT...

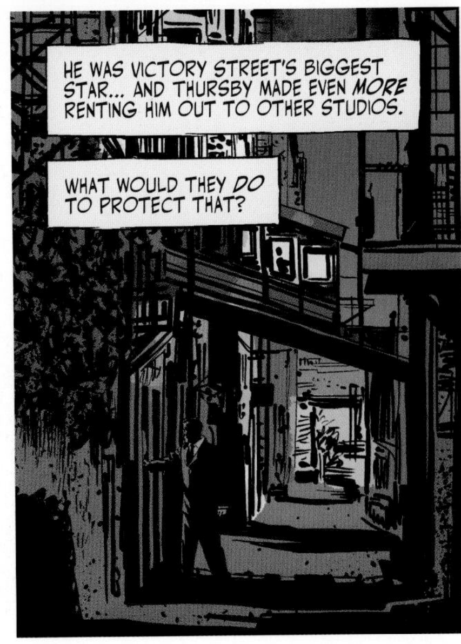
HE WAS VICTORY STREET'S BIGGEST STAR... AND THURSBY MADE EVEN *MORE* RENTING HIM OUT TO OTHER STUDIOS.
WHAT WOULD THEY *DO* TO PROTECT THAT?

BUT IT DIDN'T FIT... AND NOT JUST BECAUSE HE DOESN'T WANT TO *BELIEVE* IT.
NO, THE PROBLEM IS - WHY *NOW*?
VAL DIED A *MONTH* AGO. WHY IS BRODSKY SUDDENLY ASKING QUESTIONS NOW?
IT'S RIGHT THEN THAT HE SEES THE CRUMPLED PAPER ON THE FLOOR.
AND SOMEHOW...
HE JUST *KNOWS*.
OH... SHIT...
If you don't want the
truth about Valeria
Sommers death to come
out, put $1000 dollars
ni a ba gg
FUCKIN' GIL... HE'S *ALWAYS* BEEN A TERRIBLE TYPIST.

End of Act Two

The covers from original serialization

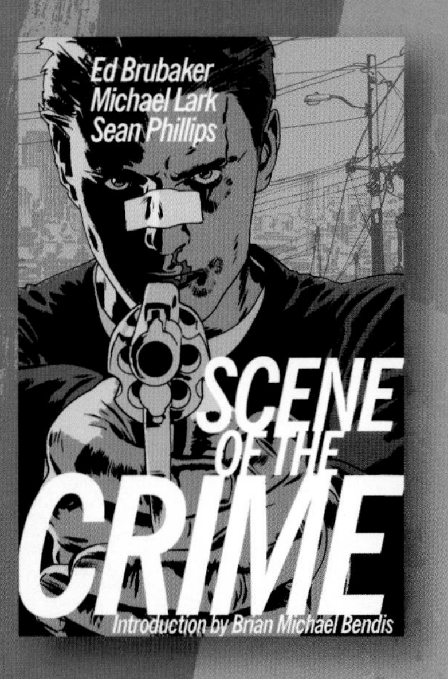

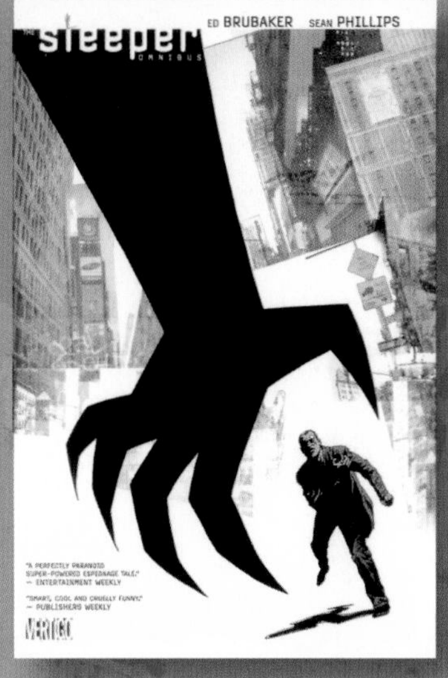

Ed Brubaker
Sean Phillips
CRIMINAL
Coward

Ed Brubaker
Sean Phillips
CRIMINAL
Lawless

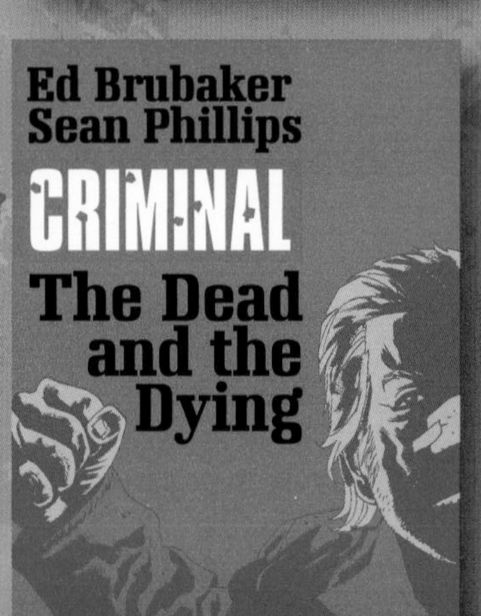

Ed Brubaker
Sean Phillips
CRIMINAL
Bad Night

Ed Brubaker
Sean Phillips
CRIMINAL
The Sinners

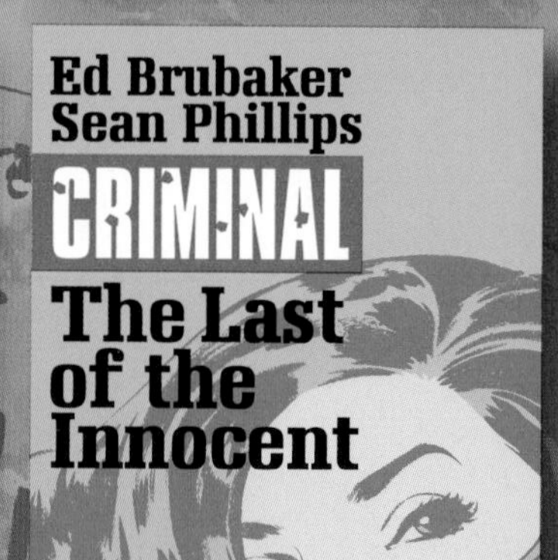

ED BRUBAKER
SEAN PHILLIPS
INCOGNITO
THE CLASSIFIED EDITION
INCOGNITO

"Ed Brubaker and Sean Phillips have earned a place among the classic partnerships in comic books."
- AV Club

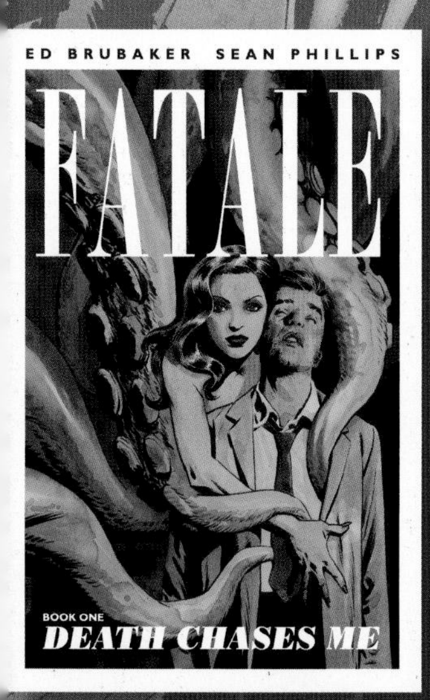
ED BRUBAKER SEAN PHILLIPS
FATALE
BOOK ONE
DEATH CHASES ME

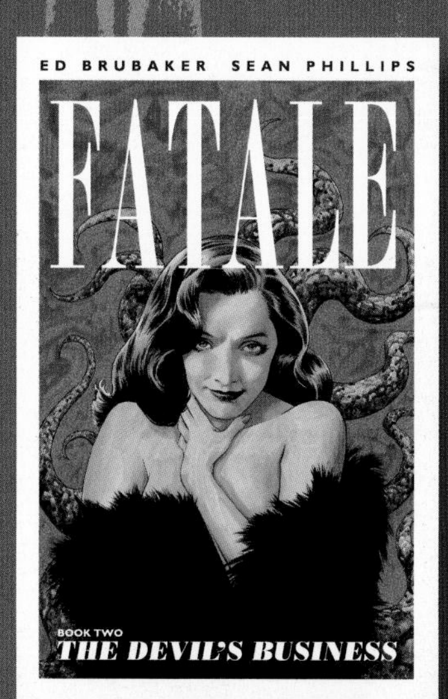
ED BRUBAKER SEAN PHILLIPS
FATALE
BOOK TWO
THE DEVIL'S BUSINESS

ED BRUBAKER SEAN PHILLIPS
FATALE
BOOK THREE
WEST OF HELL

ED BRUBAKER SEAN PHILLIPS
FATALE
BOOK FOUR
PRAY FOR RAIN

ED BRUBAKER SEAN PHILLIPS
FATALE
BOOK FIVE
CURSE THE DEMON

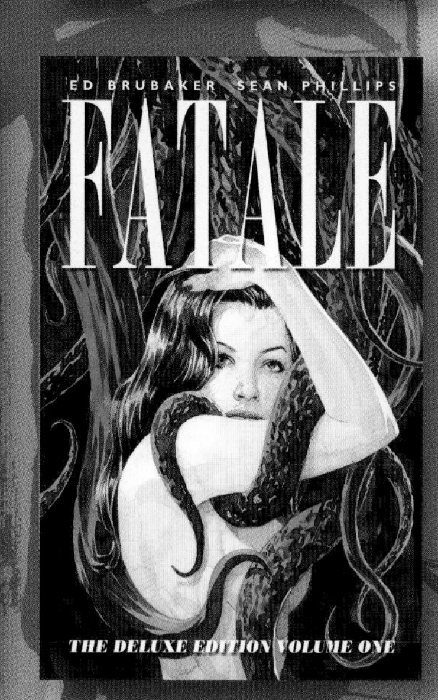
ED BRUBAKER SEAN PHILLIPS
FATALE
THE DELUXE EDITION VOLUME ONE

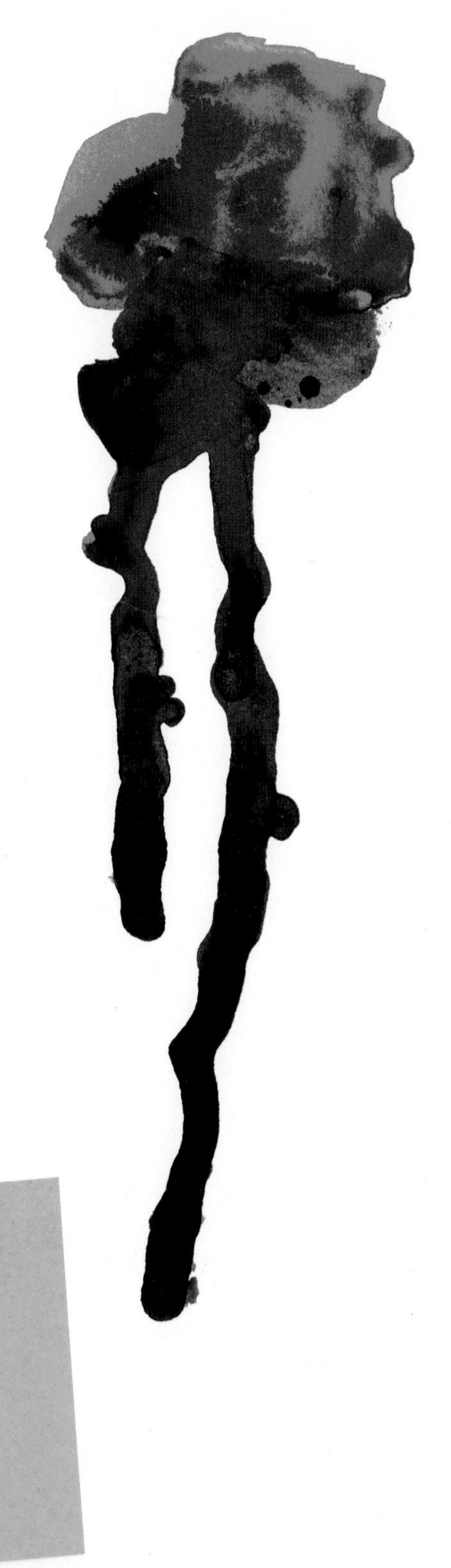